First Facts®

UNEXPLAINED MYSTERIES

The Unsolved Mystery of the LOCH NESS MONSTER

by Terri Sievert

First Facts are published by Capstone Press,
1710 Roe Crest Drive, North Mankato, Minnesota 56003
www.capstonepub.com

Library of Congress Cataloging-in-Publication Data
Sievert, Terri.
   The unsolved mystery of the Loch Ness monster / by Terri Sievert.
       p. cm. — (First facts. Unexplained mysteries)
   Summary: "Presents the legend of the Loch Ness monster, including current theories and famous sightings"—Provided by publisher.
   Includes bibliographical references and index.
   ISBN 978-1-62065-133-9 (library binding)
   ISBN 978-1-62065-810-9 (paperback)
   ISBN 978-1-4765-1066-8 (eBook PDF)
   1. Loch Ness monster—Juvenile literature. I. Title.
   QL89.2.L6S544 2013
   001.944—dc23   2012028438

Editorial Credits
Mari Bolte, editor; Veronica Correia, designer; Wanda Winch, media researcher,
Jennifer Walker, production specialist

Photo Credits
© Lee Krystek, 2007, 11; Dreamstime: Victor Habbick, 15; Getty Images Inc.: Victor Habbick Visions, 9; iStockphoto: Matt Craven, 20; Newscom: Mirrorpix/Academy of Applied Science, Boston, MA, 16, Zuma Press, 12; Shutterstock: Catmando, 18-19, Jeff Banke, 6, Ralf Juergen Kraft, cover (monster), sgrigor, background, Victor Habbick, 4

Printed in China.
092012   006936RRDS13

0 1021 0277738 4

Table of Contents

Chapter 1

People sometimes call the Loch Ness Monster "Nessie."

A Creature in the Lake

A shadow moves across the cold, dark waters of **Loch** Ness. The water ripples. Suddenly something large breaks the surface of the water. Could it be the Loch Ness Monster? Some people believe a strange creature lives deep in the Scottish lake.

loch—the Scottish word for lake

Chapter 2

At least 4,000 sightings of the Loch Ness Monster have been reported.

History and Legend

Loch Ness is a long, deep lake in Scotland. Could there be a monster living beneath the water? No one knows for sure. But there have been thousands of sightings. People claim to have seen a strange beast both in and out of the water.

In 1880 Duncan McDonald dived into Loch Ness to study a shipwreck. He claimed he saw an evil-looking monster deep in the lake.

Many people say they've seen a creature with a long neck and a tiny head. Some say the animal has humps on its back. Still others claim Nessie has flippers instead of legs.

Stories of the Loch Ness Monster go back 1,500 years.

In the 1930s, a new road was built next to Loch Ness. More people reported seeing Nessie. Two people saw a monster wandering across the road. The creature was seen holding a small animal in its mouth.

One report tells of an animal with a long neck, a thick body, and four flippers. Another tale tells of a huge animal that rolled and dived in the water.

11

In 1960 a Nessie hunter claimed to have taken a picture of the monster. The photo showed a dark object swimming across the loch. The object was larger than any known animal living in the lake. What is Nessie?

In 1931 Dr. Robert Wilson snapped a picture of a monster rising out of Loch Ness.

True or False?

Some people think Robert Wilson's famous photo of Nessie was faked. But is Nessie real?

True:

- Sightings of Nessie have been reported since AD 565.

- Other videos and photographs have been taken of the monster.

False:

- In 1994 Wilson's stepson claimed the photo was really of a toy submarine.

- Other people have played Loch Ness Monster **hoaxes**. In 1933 someone made fake footprints around the loch. People thought the footprints belonged to Nessie.

hoax—a trick to make people believe something that is not true

Chapter 3

Nessie or Not?

Some people think Nessie is a **plesiosaur**. Others think she could be an elephant swimming underwater. Some believe Nessie is a whale, a seal, or a large fish. **Skeptics** say the sightings were just floating logs or boats.

plesiosaur—a large swimming reptile that lived during the time of the dinosaurs

skeptic—a person who questions things that other people believe in

Plesiosaurs lived 65 to 200 million years ago. But Loch Ness formed only 10,000 years ago.

Chapter 4

Searching for Nessie

Many people travel to Scotland every year, hoping to see Nessie. They bring cameras, boats, and other special equipment to help their search.

The first **sonar** image of Nessie was taken in the early 1970s.

True or False?

Can special equipment
help scientists find Nessie?

True:

- In 1972 scientists used an underwater camera to look in the lake. One picture showed a flipper-shaped object.

- In 1987 scientists used sonar to try and find Nessie. The sonar showed three large objects in Loch Ness.

False:

- No Nessie bones have ever been found.

- Nessie hasn't been caught on film since 1992.

sonar—a device that uses sound waves to find underwater objects; sonar stands for sound navigation and ranging

Other water monsters have been spotted around the world. The Mokele-mbembe is a dinosaur-like lake monster believed to live in Africa. Creatures called Burus may have scaly skin and short spikes. They are said to live in the swamps of India. But like Nessie, nobody has ever proved these mysterious creatures exist.

Tales of sea dragons like the Loch Ness monster have been told around the world.

Is the Loch Ness Monster real? Some people believe Nessie exists. They think the sightings and photos are enough evidence. Others need bones and physical proof to believe. Until the mystery is solved, what swims in Loch Ness will remain unknown.

Glossary

hoax (HOHKS)—a trick to make people believe something that is not true

loch (LAHK)—the Scottish word for lake

plesiosaur (PLEE-see-uh-sohr)—a large swimming reptile that lived during the time of the dinosaurs

skeptic (SKEP-tik)—a person who questions things that other people believe in

sonar (SOH-nar)—a device that uses sound waves to find underwater objects; sonar stands for sound navigation and ranging.

Read More

Roberts, Steven. *The Loch Ness Monster!* Jr. Graphic Monster Stories. New York: PowerKids Press, 2013.

Schach, David. *The Loch Ness Monster.* The Unexplained. Minneapolis: Bellwether Media, 2011.

Troupe, Thomas Kingsley *The Legend of the Loch Ness Monster.* Legend Has It. Mankato, Minn.: Picture Window Books, 2012.

Internet Sites

FactHound offers a safe, fun way to find Internet sites related to this book. All of the sites on FactHound have been researched by our staff.

Here's all you do:

Visit *www.facthound.com*

Type in this code: 9781620651339

Super-cool stuff! Check out projects, games and lots more at
www.capstonekids.com

Index